Elegant Silhouettes of the Twenties

EDITED BY
Bonnie Welch

DOVER PUBLICATIONS, INC.
NEW YORK

Published in Canada by General Publishing Company, Ltd., 30 Lesmill Road, Don Mills, Toronto, Ontario.
Published in the United Kingdom by Constable and Company, Ltd.

Elegant Silhouettes of the Twenties is a new work, first published by Dover Publications, Inc., in 1987.

DOVER *Pictorial Archive* SERIES

Manufactured in the United States of America
Dover Publications, Inc., 31 East 2nd Street, Mineola, N.Y. 11501

Library of Congress Cataloging-in-Publication Data

Elegant silhouettes of the twenties.

(Dover pictorial archive series)
1. Silhouettes—Germany—Themes, motives. I. Welch, Bonnie. II. Series.
NC910.2.G3E44 1987   736'.98   87-13495
ISBN 0-486-25502-6 (pbk.)

PUBLISHER'S NOTE

THE SILHOUETTE has long been a popular form of representation and decoration. Thought to have had its origins in the outline and shadow paintings and drawings of Paleolithic cave muralists, silhouette art gained prominence in many ancient cultures, including those of Greece, Rome, Egypt and China. It reached the height of its popularity in the West during the eighteenth and nineteenth centuries, when it became a fashionable means of household ornamentation among the aristocracy and a fanciful means of inexpensive portraiture among the middle and lower classes. (The name by which we now know these painted or paper-cut shadow portraits and scenes was derived from the name of the notoriously frugal mid-eighteenth-century French minister of finance, Etienne de Silhouette, who amused himself by cutting out paper profiles of his contemporaries.) The production of silhouettes continued into the first half of the twentieth century, albeit on a somewhat smaller (though technically advanced) scale owing primarily to the rise in popularity of photography. Today, after a short period of neglect, silhouettes have once again become a highly regarded and popular form of art, particularly among graphic artists, designers, illustrators and craftspeople, who have found that the silhouette's versatility, adaptability, old-fashioned charm and traditional appeal make it ideal for many uses.

Especially prized by contemporary silhouette admirers and users are those elaborate, extraordinarily delicate and artistically precise die-cut silhouettes that were manufactured in Europe in the 1920s. This volume presents 57 such silhouettes, reproduced directly from an extremely rare collection of superbly made German die-cuts. Reflecting the carefree fantasies of a war-weary world, the designs depict romantic young lovers magnificently attired in fine fashions reminiscent of the eighteenth and nineteenth centuries, lads and lassies at play in their chic modern garb, cupids serenading and wood nymphs prancing, fabulous galleons in full sail, tranquil Venetian scenes and much, much more. Throughout, regardless of the variety of period dress, the mood is strictly that of the Twenties, eminently whimsical and profoundly elegant.

Copyright-free, these silhouettes lend themselves to a multiplicity of uses. They can be mounted and framed for display on a wall, as they probably would have been by their original purchasers. They can also be used to adorn greeting cards, stationery and menus, or for decoupage, book and package design or any type of needlework or other craft project. Of course, they can also be enjoyed simply for their time-less beauty and artistic merit. So whether you are just browsing idly, studying pre-Art Deco twentieth-century illustration, or hunting for the perfect design to fill a graphic need, the graceful yet bold images in this book will surely demonstrate to you why the silhouette has long been such a popular and useable art form.

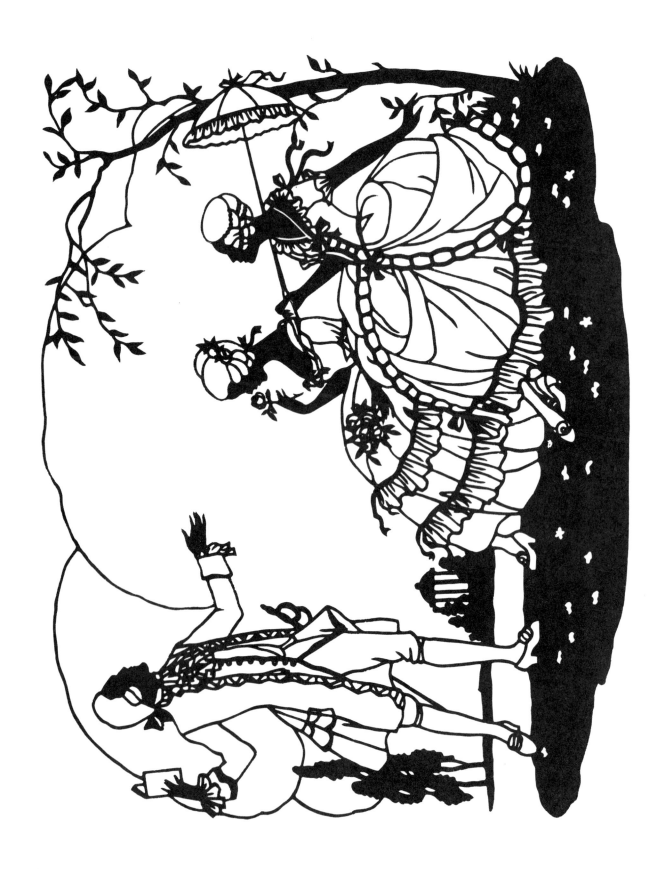